When A Child Goes To Heaven

By Scott & Cheri Scheer

Copyright © 1998 "Rebecca's Footprint"
Christian Family Ministries
Copyright © 2003 Family Ministries, Inc.

All rights reserved

Scriptures from the King James Version

*Special thanks to Rochelle Fenlason (Rebecca's Mom)
for her help, strength and encouragement
in completing this book.*

**Family Ministries, Inc.
Lake Junaluska, NC USA**
www.familyministries.net

Cover by Jeff Martens

Printed by Faith printing in the United Sates of America

DEDICATION

This book is dedicated to the memory of Rebecca Marie Fenlason and all the babies who are now in heaven. They continue to live on in the hearts and memories of the families who love them.

This book is also dedicated to the friends and family members who sent cards and flowers, prayed, shed tears, and shared encouragement.

And most of all, this book is dedicated to our Lord Jesus Christ, who remains a faithful and merciful God, despite our weaknesses and mistakes; in whom we can trust because of His love and His strength that endures forever and ever.

WHEN A CHILD GOES TO HEAVEN

By Scott and Cheri Scheer

Preface

If you walked into the Scheer's office, you would see many pictures of their family. Some members live in distant states. Some of those shown in the photos are older now and need an updated picture! The children have grown – their two daughters are now married and their son is now a minister, following in Pastor Scheer's footsteps. One tender addition to the great wall of pictures is an imprint of two tiny feet alongside a picture of their baby granddaughter, Rebecca Marie Fenlason. Her story, like her life, is brief but significant. And if you listen carefully as you read her story, you will hear God speaking to your heart.

WHEN A CHILD GOES TO HEAVEN

One of the greatest love stories ever told is that of Rebekah and Isaac. The Genesis account of Rebekah's life is surrounded in romance, wonder and intrigue. This Mesopotamian beauty has captured the attention of artists and psalmists throughout history. Her sense of kindness and grace with a willingness to fulfill the will of God immortalizes her as one of the most godly women in the Bible. Isaac, her Prince Charming, waits, longing for his bride to arrive. As an expectant mother waits with anxious anticipation for the birth of her child, so he waited. What will she look like? What new dimension will her life add to his?

Jarred and Rochelle had a romance made in heaven – like Prince Charming and Cinderella. Some called them *Ken and Barbie*. They both overflowed with talents and abilities and were blessed with an attractive appearance. There was, and still is, an aura surrounding them that distinguished them as blessed of the Lord.

They were part of the righteous generation. Both have come from a godly heritage and were reared in the things of God. They grew up learning to submit to and trust in the Lord. As youngsters they served the Lord, never knowing a time separated from Him. Their obedience to parents and the Word of God immersed them in innocence and purity. Their courtship and subsequent marriage were seasoned with a desire for the perfect will of God in their lives. Their godly lifestyle was the inspiration behind the video series The Bonding Process, which presents a godly approach to sex, dating and relationships, and was produced for the *Christian Family Values* television broadcast.

Eleazer, the trusted servant of Abraham, was given the task of finding a wife for Isaac. He knew she would have to be special, as God had a special call upon Isaac's life. He trusted in the Spirit's leading, knowing he carried out a divine appointment. Isaac means 'laughter,' but for Isaac there hadn't been much laughter since the death of his beloved mother. His future wife would bring joy back into his life and touch many other lives as well.

~ ~ ~

Jarred and Rochelle were full of the joy of the Lord. Their faith, deep love for one another and relaxed approach to life brought happiness to all who came in contact with them. Joy had especially been evident during the first few months of Rochelle's first pregnancy. It had been almost four years since their fairytale wedding. In that time they were able to establish a successful business and settle into their own home. They desired to get things in order before having a child, and the Lord granted them their desires. Feeling that their relationship was solid and their finances in order, the energy, prayers, excitement and preparation of parents, grandparents and family had been directed towards this unborn child. Everyone knew that a precious child would surely come from this special couple. The anointing and call upon their lives would surely produce an exceptional child, *a divine appointment*.

Seventeen weeks into the pregnancy, parents, grandparents and Rochelle's sister and brother squeezed into an ultrasound room to get a first peek at *Precious*. They called the baby *Precious* (the baby's temporary name–created by Jarred's dad) rather than 'junior' or 'the baby.' Webster's definition of precious is "something of great price."

As they received the first images of this gift of great price, they stood in awe of the creative miracle. They saw tiny fingers and toes and a little heart beating in perfect rhythm. The technician said it looked like a girl, who appeared perfect in every way. There was never a question in the family's mind as to the perfect wholeness of *Precious*, but the ultrasound report helped bring a certain peace.

~ ~ ~

After a long trip across the desert from Canaan, Eleazer came to an oasis. "Surely there will be water there for me to quench my thirst," he thought. As he approached the well of Nahor, he noticed some women watering their flocks. "Could this be God's appointed time to bring the miracle of his precious chosen bride for Isaac," he wondered? One young woman in particular caught his eye; Rebekah was her name. From first glance her beauty was etched upon his mind. Because of the sign which he asked of the Lord, Eleazer asked her for a drink. She responded by not only offering him a drink, but by watering his camels as well.

~ ~ ~

Everything in Rochelle's pregnancy had been done by the book. She followed all the medical guidelines for vitamins, diet, exercise, pre-natal care, listening to the proper music and reading Scripture to the baby forming within her. Every checkup had shown a healthy baby and mother. Of course, everyone was excited to hear the little heartbeat, which we were told was normal and strong at every checkup.

During Rochelle's 36 week exam, there was concern about the baby's position and an ultrasound was ordered. Everything seemed normal, except for a possible slight abnormality that had appeared in the heart.

The doctor recommended another ultrasound, that would be preformed by a specialist with the latest scientific ultrasound technology.

That Monday, Jarred and Rochelle and Rochelle's parents took the hour-long drive to see the specialist. The doctor spent the first half hour elaborating on the difficulty of detecting heart problems through ultrasound that late into the pregnancy. An amniocentesis was recommended, along with an immediate appointment with a neonatal pediatric cardiologist.

On Tuesday, another hour-long drive was made to the appointment for the amniocentesis. Then a third drive on Wednesday was in order for the pediatric cardiologist.

The third appointment with the cardiologist finally unraveled some of the unanswered questions for Jarred and Rochelle. The tests had detected two small holes in the baby's heart and also a smaller-than-usual left ventricle chamber.

Despite the unexpected bad news, the doctor was very encouraging. She stated that a natural delivery should not be a problem and that sometime between the fourth and sixth month of life the child would need heart surgery. She seemed confident that one surgery would correct the problem and that the child would lead a normal life.

At church that evening the congregation prayed, and word went out to family and friends. Jarred and Rochelle were unmoved by this report and remained secure in their trust in God and excitement over this baby.

Exhausted from the days of tests, Rochelle went to bed early. At one in the morning she was awakened by her water breaking, and the phone call went out to the grandparents – Rochelle's water had broken and they were on their way to the birthing center. Katie, the midwife, drove with them to the local hospital. From there, they were referred to a hospital that specialized in neonatal care. As Rochelle's parents drove the couple to the specialized hospital, which was an hour away, prayer and praises filled their van. Their faith and concerns were given over to the Lord.

Even though Rochelle was three weeks early, she was still within her 'safe date.' No one seemed concerned about any complications, but to be on the safe side, they felt it was best to have care available for the baby if necessary. Rochelle was so excited. She could hardly sleep the last few hours of the night at the hospital. By 10:00 a.m. the contractions began coming five to six minutes apart. The nurses were continually commenting on how strong the baby's heartbeat was and how it was handling the stress of the contractions just fine. By 6:00 p.m. the contractions were growing in intensity, and the grandfathers and the two uncles were asked to vacate the room.

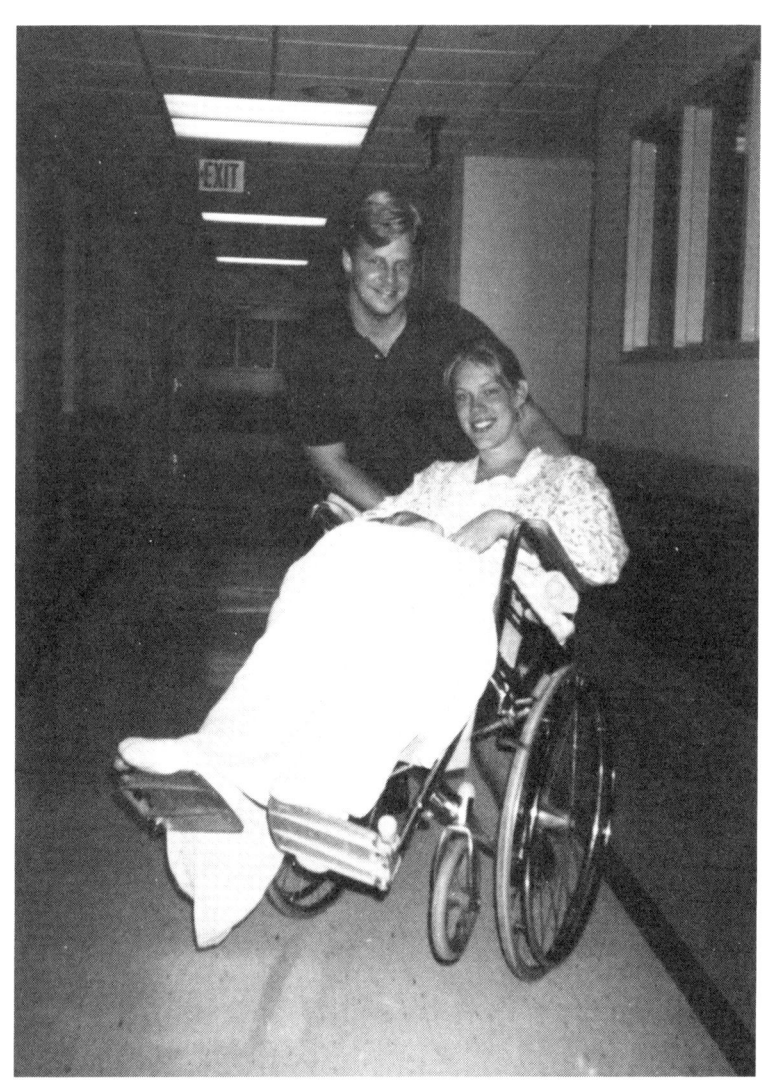

~ ~ ~

Rebekah was an extraordinary person. Her warmth and willingness to help a stranger showed exceptional character. When Eleazer shared his mission, Rebekah immediately seized the challenge with a willingness to do the will of God. There was no whining or lamenting over leaving her family. She faced the future with excitement and joyful expectation.

~ ~ ~

Rochelle has a spirit of excellence which she acquired from her mother. She has always given her all and done an excellent job in everything she has ever attempted. From her school work, to her job, to her marriage, it was always done right. Giving birth was no exception. She did it with a style all her own. She complimented her husband, thanked the nurses and doctors, and encouraged onlookers. The coaches, her mom and husband, were her greatest encouragers. As she made transition to delivery, the neonatal specialists arrived on the scene to attend to the baby's needs.

Between contractions, she greeted new participants. As the grandfathers paced and prayed outside the delivery room, they heard Rochelle say, "Isn't she beautiful; that wasn't so bad. I can't wait for the next one!" The doctors laughed and one mentioned that he had never heard anyone handle the birthing process with such exuberance.

Jarred and Rochelle named their little *Precious*, "Rebecca Marie." The pediatric specialist let Rochelle briefly touch her little girl before whisking her away to the ventilator. Once Rebecca was stabilized and her color returned to normal, she was placed in an isolette and moved to NICU for further examination.

As the isolette sped away, the grandfathers stole a look at their new granddaughter and asked the doctor about the baby's condition. The doctor said she came through the birth just fine, was a little small and needed help breathing, but appeared fine so far. They wouldn't know for sure until they performed the echo cardiogram and did further tests.

My sheep hear my voice, and I know them, and they follow me:

And I give unto them eternal life and they shall never perish, neither shall any man pluck them out of my Father's hand.

I and my Father are one.

John 10:27-30

It wasn't long until the family was allowed back in Rochelle's room. This was a time of rejoicing and thanksgiving for the blessing of this birth. Rochelle glowed with her new motherhood and the reward of bringing forth a new life into this world. Jarred, sitting by her side on the bed, smiled with the serene pride and fulfillment of a new father.

~ ~ ~

*How did Rebekah so quickly recognize the will of God for her life and so readily accept it? Eleazer, a dusty old nomad whom she didn't know at all, told her of his mission; but how did she know **she** was the one God was calling to be Isaac's wife? She must have ascertained that if she left with Eleazer, she might never see her family again. Her parents didn't seem excited over this news. But Rebekah was excited and anxious to get going, even though the family coaxed her to stay a while longer.*

~ ~ ~

Within an hour, the family was huddled outside the NICU, trying to get a glimpse of Rebecca.

Everyone wanted information from the doctors. When the doctor finally appeared, he asked to see Jarred privately. From the window, the family could see Rebecca in the isolette with an IV, respirator, and various monitor hookups. Standing next to her was her handsome daddy in serious discussion with the doctor.

After his discussion with the doctor, Jarred came out and said he wanted a few minutes alone with Rochelle. Everyone sensed that the doctor's report was not good, but had no idea what the "not good" they were sensing meant.

When the rest of the family was allowed into Rochelle's room, the glow that had been in the room right after Rebecca's birth was no longer there. Several medical personnel–including the pediatric cardiologist–entered the room and helped explain Rebecca's condition.

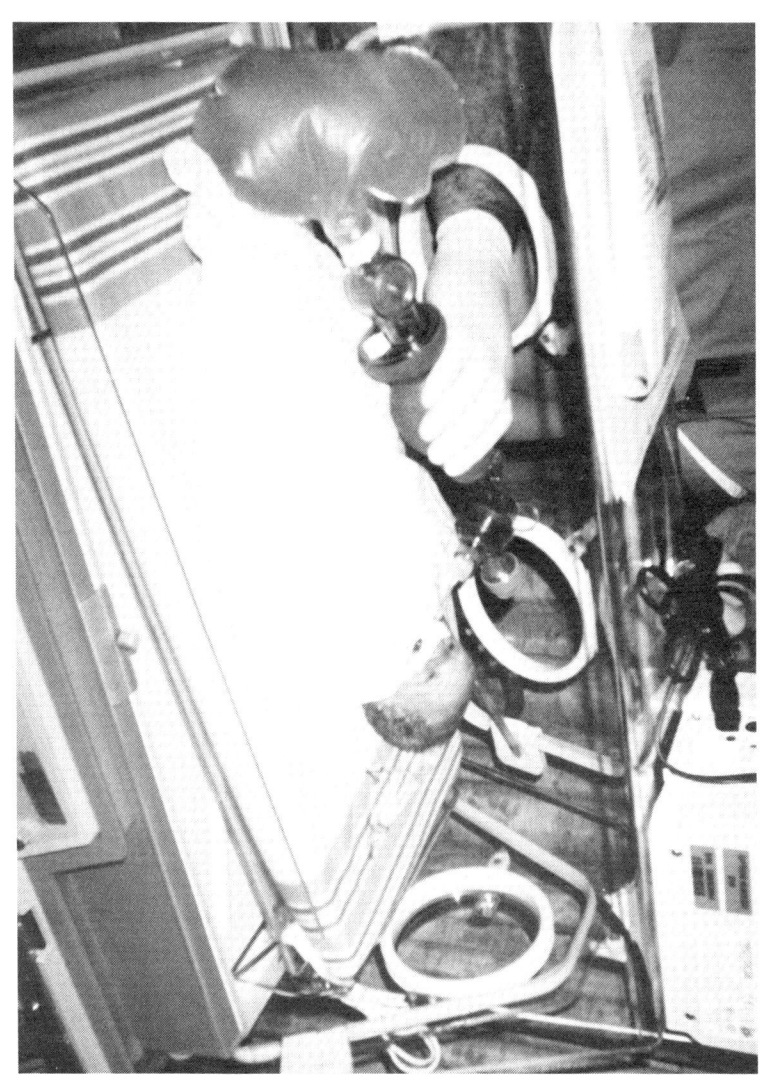

Her heart was 'hypo-plastic' and was damaged beyond what the prenatal ultrasound had shown. They suspected she had a genetic abnormality called *trisomy eighteen*. They explained that usually these babies are miscarried early in the pregnancy, or are stillborn. In the rare event when babies with Rebecca's circumstances are born alive, seldom do they live more than several days. The medical report concluded that there was nothing that could be done to save her life.

The medical team reassured us all that they would do everything possible to keep Rebecca comfortable and alive as long as feasible. With that, the doctors left the room. The tears flowed as Jarred, Rochelle and the grandparents digested the news. Could this be the will of God? This child was prayed for even before conception. Every day Jarred had laid hands upon Rochelle's tummy and prayed for *Precious*. The grandparents, parents and friends had immersed this pregnancy in prayer.

What about *"I am the God that healeth thee,"* and *"By His stripes we are healed?"* There needs to be a miracle here, Lord!

The nursery was all decorated. The baby shower was just last week. The cute little dresses were hanging in the closet, ready to be worn. Rochelle and Jarred's bedroom furniture has been rearranged to accommodate a rocker and the cradle, which was set up next to Jarred and Rochelle's bed. The safety gate was already secured in the nursery doorway to keep out Kaley, their dog. The family, the house, and everyone's hearts were ready for this new baby.

Finally, the family was allowed to go into the NICU and see their precious Rebecca. It was so hard to comprehend that this beautiful little baby was the one spoken of in the doctor's report. She was so active, with arms and legs in motion. The family could pick out the distinctive features . . . she had Mommy's nose and toes . . . definitely Daddy's lips.

Nevertheless I am continually with thee: thou hast holden me in thy right hand.

Thou shalt guide me with thy counsel, and afterward receive me to glory.

Whom have I in heaven but thee? And there is none upon the earth that I desire beside thee.

My flesh and my heart faileth; but God is the strength of my heart, and my portion forever.

For, lo, they that are far from thee shall perish: thou hast destroyed all them that go a whoring from thee.

But it is good to draw near to God; I have put my trust in the Lord GOD, that I may declare all thy works.

Psalm 73:23-28

Rebecca grabbed Grandpa's finger and held tight. Grandpa dispelled the thought that he may never hold her hand for a walk in the park. Rochelle and her mom stood there reaching into the isolette, caressing Rebecca's arms, legs, and body, just wanting to hold her close.

Rebekah's family threw a great party and invited their friends and relatives. There was much merriment and rejoicing as the godly family accepted God's plan for their Rebekah. Their rejoicing in the faithfulness of God to carry out His will for their daughter was, however, mixed with the sorrow of knowing she was going to a faraway land. It might be a long time before they would see her again.

Friday morning brought with it a new report from the specialist. He informed the family that it was a miracle Rebecca had even made it through the night; there was much more wrong with her than was earlier reported.

He suggested that they all make the most of whatever time was left with Rebecca. With that report, and despite the fact that the doctor said Rebecca needed constant monitoring and care by trained medical personnel, Jarred and Rochelle requested that Rebecca be brought into their room.

Around 10:00 a.m. Rebecca was ushered into the room by two nurses who were assisting with her life support. Could it be possible that this beautiful, prayed-for, dedicated to the Lord from conception child was leaving so soon? Her parents and family had already envisioned a lifetime of memories yet to be made. Would God in some incomprehensible, sovereign plan allow this life to touch the other lives of this planet for only such a short time?

Rochelle's father performed the baptism and pronounced a blessing over his beautiful granddaughter. The family then took turns holding Rebecca. She was kissed, talked to, sang to, and prayed over. No one wanted to give her up. They all had so many things planned for her and with her. This family knew the power of prayer, the meaning of faith, and how to trust God. They all shared personal testimonies of how God had divinely intervened in each of their lives at one time or another. As the minutes passed there was still the expectation of a miracle. There was also an awareness of peace and God's grace . . . preparing the family for whatever was about to take place.

Rochelle held Rebecca most of the time, memorizing a picture of her sweet little face, and forming a vivid memory of what it felt like to touch her soft skin and fine hair. Rochelle herself was cradled in the arms of her loving husband, Jarred. Rochelle spoke tenderly to her daughter, *"Daddy and Mommy love you so much, Rebecca. We're the ones who have been telling you about Jesus for the past eight months. All these people here love you. Your Grandmas and Grandpas and your aunts and uncles are here because you're such a special part of our lives."*

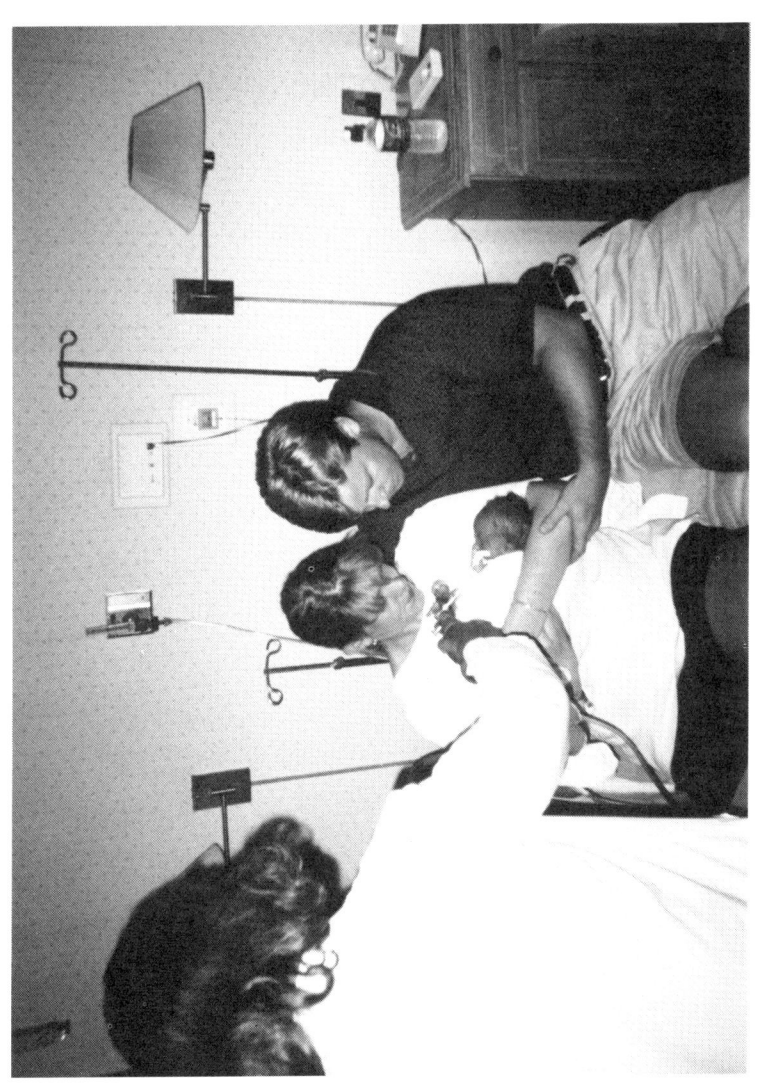

Then Rochelle sang to Rebecca the same song Rochelle's mom used to sing to her:

*I am Jesus' little lamb,
Ever glad at heart I am;
Jesus loves and gently guides me;
Knows my needs and well provides me;
Loves me every day the same,
Even calls me by my name.*

It was two in the afternoon when Rebecca's pastor-grandpa performed the baptism/dedication service. Everyone prayed and thanked God for His hand upon their lives and upon Rebecca. Jarred said it best as he prayed, *"Father, we thank you for Rebecca and the time we have had with her. We place her in Your hands for Your will to be done."* After that, Rebecca became very peaceful and quiet.

At 2:29 p.m., Rebecca Marie Fenlason went to be with Jesus. At that moment, the attending physician checked her heart and announced, "She's gone to heaven."

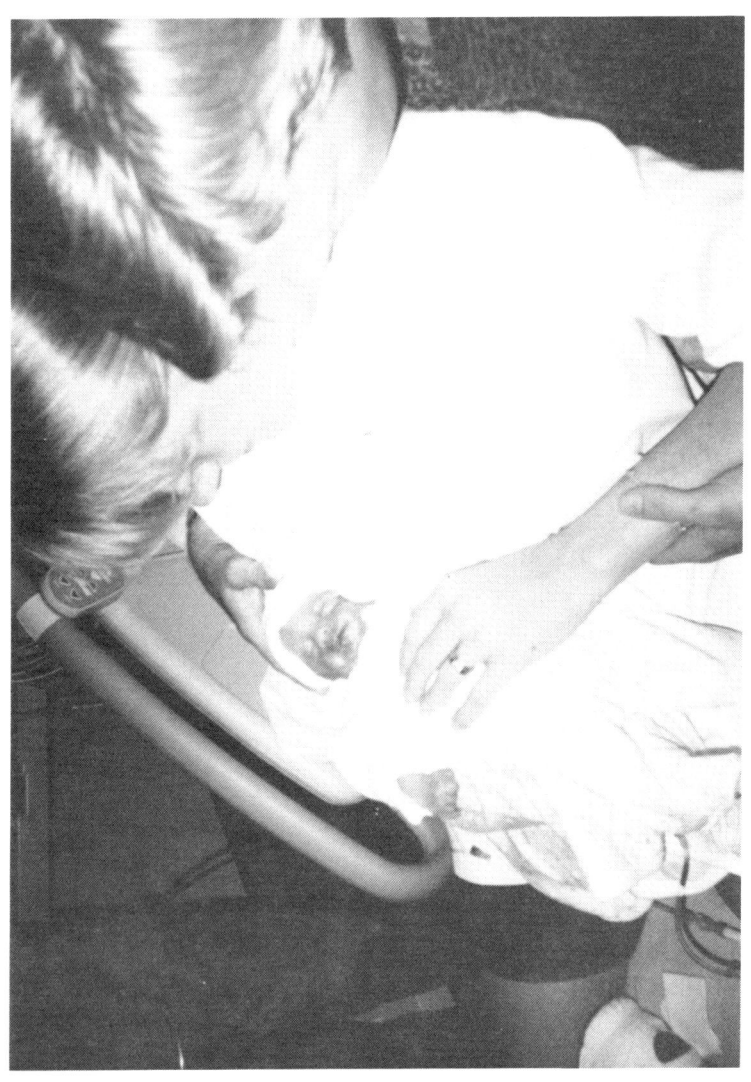

A greater peace came over the room, and, for that moment, the sorrow was somewhat lifted as that precious soul entered her heavenly home.

~ ~ ~

Rebekah said her goodbyes, then mounted a camel and left with the servant Eleazer. There was an excitement and anticipation as she headed across the wilderness to meet her husband-to-be. Isaac waited in earnest, praying to God for Eleazer's success. Suddenly, he saw the caravan. Could it be Eleazer? Yes, it was, and there was a woman with him! Upon spotting the man who must be Isaac, Rebekah dismounted her camel and ran to greet him.

~ ~ ~

For a short time, Rochelle continued to hold Rebecca's lifeless body. There was a serenity in the room as different family members contemplated the reality of the moment. As Rebecca was being received into the loving arms of the Lord Jesus, her parents, grandparents and extended family were all envisioning the joy of the heavenly hosts as they received another precious soul into heaven. They could even envision family members who had gone on before greeting Rebecca as she was ushered into the very presence of God: Jarred's grandmother and his brother Jeff; Rochelle's Grandpa Cavanaugh and Uncle Tommy; and Rebecca's namesake, Great-grandma Marie. Rebecca would no doubt have many arms to embrace and comfort her. And they thought about the future, when they would all see Rebecca again as they entered the heavenly gates.

Her eighteen hours on earth were wrought with pain, confusion, poking, prodding, and discomfort. But as she entered heaven, she was whole, breathing on her own, never to know pain again. She would never sleep in the beautiful nursery her family had prepared for her, but what was that compared to the heavenly nursery which her Father God had prepared for her?

Rebekah and Isaac found love and comfort in their God-ordained relationship. God blessed their relationship with a pregnancy. Rebekah felt a struggle inside her and sought the Lord concerning it. The lord told her she was carrying twins and that the two would be at odds with one

another: one son – blessed of the Lord, and one son – a rough and violent man.

~ ~ ~

There was an emotional struggle as each family member accessed their loss. The months of waiting were now over. So much preparation, anticipation, and prayer had been poured over this little one. What *about* the prayers, Lord? The whole family had been praying since Rebecca's conception. Every day her daddy had laid hands on her mommy's tummy and dedicated Rebecca's life and development to God. Where was the justice in this world? Rebecca had shared the NICU with crack-cocaine babies and babies with other physical ailments whose mothers didn't seem to care if their babies lived or died. But this family wanted their Rebecca.

Everyone shared the sentiment that *it's not right to go through pregnancy and delivery and leave the hospital without a baby.* The question "why" was avoided for the time-being. Though the grief and sorrow were real, there was a certain peace and understanding that God had everything under control. Like the story of Shadrack, Meshack, and

Abednego, Jarred and Rochelle had to walk through this 'fiery furnace,' but they were not alone. As evidenced by their countenance, demeanor and conversation, God was walking them through this. Their love and support for each other was a great encouragement to the family and an evidence of God's grace.

Rebecca went to be with the Lord the Friday before Mother's Day. That Sunday there was a heaviness in *Christian Family Church* where Jarred and Rochelle were members.

Many people there loved Jarred and Rochelle dearly and had been praying for them through this whole ordeal. Pastor Scott and Cheri Scheer, Rochelle's dad and mom, encouraged the congregation.

That Sunday's message was entitled "A Mother's Heart." Pastor Scott related how, throughout Rochelle's pregnancy, the midwives and doctors had often commented about how strong the baby's heartbeat was. Even during Rochelle's labor, the nurses said the monitors indicated a strong heartbeat. Cheri had asked the baby's heart specialist how it was that the baby's heart was so badly damaged, yet the early tests had not shown any abnormality or fetal distress? He explained that Rochelle's heart was strong, and as long as Rebecca was connected to her mother, Rochelle's heart beat for Rebecca. Any problem went unnoticed. Once Rebecca was delivered and the umbilical cord was cut, separating her from her mother's heart, she had been unable to function on her own.

This message struck home. It's the sacrificial, Christ-like heart of the mother that keeps the family, the church, and the nation together. It's the mother's heart that keeps the family going. Godly mothers and fathers must stand in faith for their marriages and their families. It has become so easy to give up when faced with disappointment or challenges. Sometimes, it's the spouse or parent who stands in the gap and hangs onto faith for a marriage or a child that provides the only hope. If we give up too easily, we may be cutting the spiritual umbilical cord that is the only source of life and hope for that spouse, that child.

In the midst of sorrow, God is faithful to lift our grieving spirits. In our disappointment, He provides hope. In a challenge, He shows a way through. As long as we are connected to God's heart, we receive life and are strong. On our own, separated from His heart, our weaknesses can be fatal, spiritually and perhaps physically.

~ ~ ~

Eleazer traveled with ten camels. These beasts of burden were laden with many gifts. There were many gifts that were given to Rebekah and to her family. The generosity of Isaac must surely have been a comfort to the family and also to Rebekah.

~ ~ ~

The gifts of God in this tragedy came in the form of people. Cards, flowers and phone calls streamed in from everywhere. The body of Christ showed its true potential in the wake of tragedy. The words of comfort and encouragement were a healing ointment to Jarred, Rochelle and the family. Many individuals and churches had activated their intercessory prayer ministries. Those prayers were definitely needed and received.

Blessed be GOD, even the Father of our LORD Jesus Christ, the Father of mercies, and the God of all comfort.

Who comforteth us in all our tribulation, that we may be able to comfort them which are in trouble, by the comfort of God.

For as the sufferings of Christ abound in us, so our consolation also aboundeth by Christ.

2 Corinthians 1:3-5

Rebecca had been born on Thursday and died on Friday. The memorial service was held on Monday. Jarred and Rochelle were strengthened by family and hundreds of friends who came to support them. Everyone who attended the memorial service was handed a bulletin entitled *"A Tribute to Rebecca Marie Fenlason."* The platform in the Christian Family Church sanctuary had been decorated with an array of floral displays sent by loved ones, and a beautiful, flourishing palm tree sent by Jarred and Rochelle's aunts, uncles, and grandparents.

In the center, on a table, sat a tiny casket, which contained the mortal remains of little Rebecca. She wore a pink and white rosebud dress that her maternal Grandma had purchased for her weeks earlier. Placed on and around the tiny little casket were some of the toys and stuffed animals that had been awaiting her. Next to the casket stood a beautiful cross, handmade by Jarred's parents, adorned with silk flowers and a banner that read "Precious."

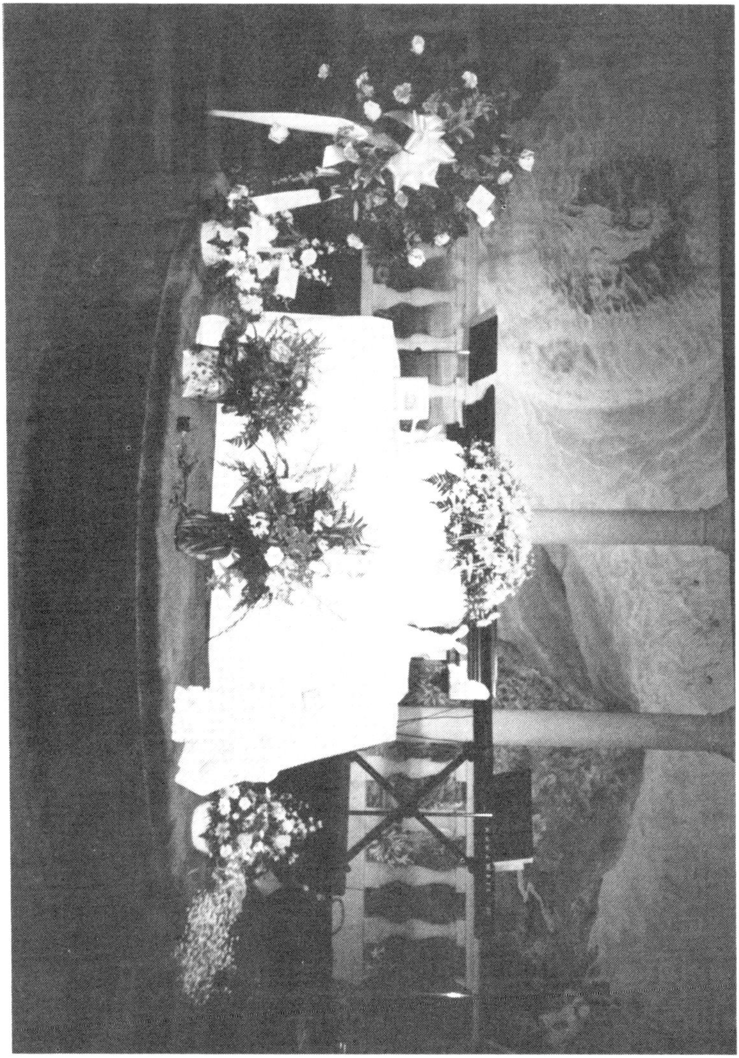

Rebecca's maternal grandpa, Pastor Scott Scheer, opened the service with a welcome and prayer. Rebecca's uncle, Pastor James Scheer, led the congregation in the singing of "How Great Thou Art," "He's More Than Wonderful," and "The Family Prayer Song." Pastor Scott read the obituary and Psalm 90, verses one through six and thirteen through seventeen.

Suzanne Fenlason, read from a special book, "Mommy and Daddy, Please Don't Cry," by Linda DeYmaz. It was written especially for parents who have lost a child. It relates the happy, joyful experiences of a child who has died and is now enjoying heaven. This brought a few smiles from the congregation as many could relate to the glorious hope of being united with those loved ones who had died and gone to heaven.

Together Jarred and Rochelle read a letter they had written to Rebecca:

To Our Precious Daughter Rebecca,

We are so proud to be your parents. We've called you "Precious" while you were in the womb because we knew you were a precious gift from God. Your birth was one of the most incredible experiences of our lives. We heard you cry for only a brief moment before we began to cry. You looked so perfect. Your skin was free from any blemish and your eyes were wide and alert. We didn't know it was going to be the last time we would hear you cry. It certainly wasn't the last time we cried. Your grandpas and grandmas and uncles and aunts did a lot of crying, too, because they love you so much. They were a big support. Someday you'll know how many people truly love you!

We never saw your smile, but we'll never forget how you looked at us. It was amazing to see how you turned your head and looked into our eyes when we would talk to you. You made us smile when you reacted with calmness to the touch of our hands and the sounds of our voices. Rebecca, we don't understand why your little heart and lungs weren't perfect, or why your life was so brief. We don't always understand God's perfect will, but we trust our Heavenly Father. We know that God is all-powerful, all-knowing, and all-loving, and that's enough. God allowed us, your earthly parents, the honor of ushering you into this life for a very short time. Now, your Heavenly Father has given you the gift of eternal life. We dedicated you to Him long before you were even born. You are truly His.

We love you so very much that our hearts ache to think of our lives without you. But we rejoice in your new life, a life that will never know pain or grief or stress. Your new body is perfect and whole. We very much look forward to the day when we can see you again.

We'll Love You Always,

Mom and Dad

47

There wasn't a dry eye in the church. For some, the tears were those of hope, to see their loved ones again someday soon. But above all, there was an admiration of the strength of this young couple. Jarred and Rochelle's words encouraged and comforted all who were there. There was a message of real hope for all and a deeper understanding of the gift of God's grace.

Pastor Scott shared five scriptures and delivered a message of life.

II Samuel 12:16-23 relates the story of King David at the loss of his infant son. King David put the situation in God's hands and went on with his life.

I Thessalonians 4:13-18 encourages Christians with the hope of Christ's return. Family members and friends will see Rebecca again and will have eternity to be with her.

Mark 10:13-16 is a precious portion of scripture which gives a picture of Jesus' love for children. The kingdom of heaven was made for Rebecca and all other children who are residents there.

Finally, Romans 8:28, "And we know that all things work together for good to them that love the Lord and are called according to His purpose." Rebecca's parents, family and the congregation were encouraged with these words: this *will* work out for good. We are called of God and are faithful to fulfill His purpose and plan in our lives.

Rochelle's mother, Cheri, shared some comforting thoughts and sang "In the Presence of Jehovah." This song describes how, in the presence of our Great God, our troubles seem to vanish and our broken hearts are mended. This song had a twofold meaning to those there as they thought about their own sadness and also about Rebecca's little heart that was now whole.

The LORD is my strength and my shield; my heart trusteth in him, and I am helped: therefore my heart greatly rejoiceth; and with my song will I praise him.
Psalm 28:7

The LORD also will be a refuge for oppressed, a refuge in times of trouble.

And they that know thy name will put their trust in thee: for thou, LORD, hast not forsaken them that seek thee.
Psalm 9:9,10

The righteous cry, and the LORD heareth, and delivers them out of all their troubles.

The LORD is nigh (near) unto them that are of a broken heart; and saveth such as be of a contrite spirit.
Psalm 34:17,18

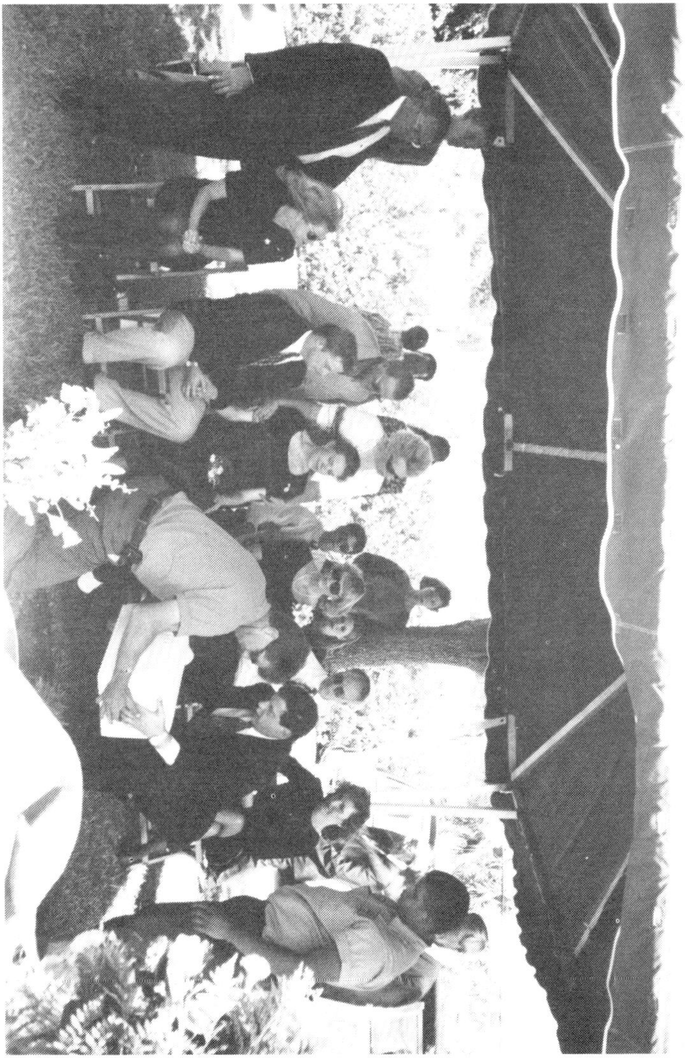

~ ~ ~

Rebekah's husband, Isaac was sick and dying, and Rebekah's precious son Jacob lived in a foreign land. She felt grief, yet there was peace and contentment. Jacob was in the plan of God. His life would beget a nation, a chosen people that would show forth the glory of God. Although she felt a sadness and loss that was very real to her, she could still feel that God was in control.

~ ~ ~

After the memorial service, the family went to the cemetery. Following a time of intimate sharing, the tiny casket was lowered into the grave. One by one, the family members dropped a flower into the grave onto the casket. Rebecca was buried near Jarred's brother Jeff, who had died of cancer at the age of eighteen, and Jarred's grandmother, who had gone home to be with the Lord only six months after Jeff.

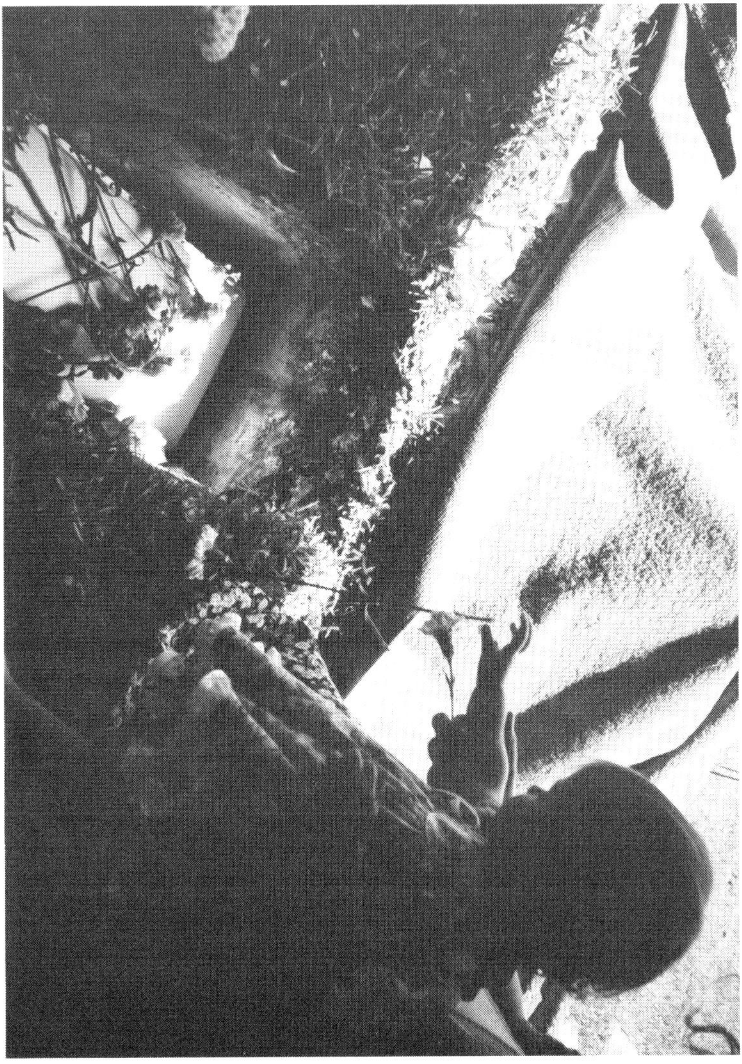

Everyone said their last *goodbyes* to Rebecca. There was a greater level of tranquility as this ritual gave finality to the whole ordeal. Now, although Rebecca was in a "foreign land," everyone felt contentment in knowing that she was in God's perfect plan in her heavenly home.

Many good things have come out of this tragedy. The testimony of God's grace, love, and comfort has been evident. One young mother related how she had been frustrated raising her children. She had lamented her role as mother. Upon hearing Rochelle's story, she asked God to forgive her for her attitude. She thanked Him for her children and her responsibilities as a mother. An unwed mother shared how she had a greater appreciation for the miracle of her healthy baby.

The family has had countless opportunities to give testimony to the goodness and faithfulness of God. All things do work together for good to those who love God!

Before Rebecca's heart stopped beating, a nurse took an ink imprint of Rebecca's footprint for the "memorial certificate." The nurse made several copies and gave them to Jarred and Rochelle before they left the hospital. Later, they added a picture of Rebecca to the certificate and gave one to each family member at the memorial service. That little footprint left an imprint on the hearts of many. As time has passed, each one has found the pain and sorrow diminishing, as the testimonies continue to come in.

Rebecca only lived on this planet for 18 ½ hours, yet she touched more lives than some people ever touch in their entire lifetime. To this very day, Jarred and Rochelle testify that trusting God means trusting His decisions, even when they are not understood or liked.

The peace and strength that have come from wholeheartedly trusting in God have been evident throughout their lives. And His Word promises that *you* can experience that same peace from knowing and trusting Him.

When thou passest through the waters, I will be with thee; and through the rivers, they shall not overflow thee: when thou walkest through the fire, thou shalt not be burned; neither shall the flame kindle upon thee.

Isaiah 43:2

There is a natural grieving process which God alludes to in Ecclesiastes 3:1&4: "There is a time for everything . . . a time to weep and a time to laugh, a time to mourn and a time to dance." (NIV)

Rochelle and Jarred found that continuing to ask "why" would not bring healing or resolution to their lives. Some things are best left unanswered in our minds. Scripture says, "Who can know the mind of God? His ways are above our ways, His thoughts are above our thoughts." Rochelle's Mom remarked on how she had learned that truly trusting God and having faith in Him meant that she could have enough faith to believe and trust Him to do what is best for her–even when it didn't seem to line up with what *she* wanted. Rather than have faith in her faith, she would have faith in her God and His ultimate plan for her good.

Some final thoughts . . .
Many cards, flowers and condolences poured in from loving family and friends across the nation. There were two cards in which Rochelle found special comfort.

The first card read:

*Find comfort in the <u>sovereignty</u> of God.
There is no lost potential,
no purpose unaccomplished;
There is only the glorious plan of God perfectly
fulfilled in a precious life.*

The second simply stated:

*Long ago and far away
Before the laws of time and space
A loving God prepared a place . . .
High above this world facade
The hope of man, the home of God . . .
Somewhere beyond all doubt and fear
Beyond the reach of sorrow's tears
Where broken hearts run strong and free
Where every child of God will be . . .*

MAY 7 - MAY 8
1998
REBECCA M. FENLASON
OUR PRECIOUS BABY DAUGHTER

If you are grieving over the loss of a child, we encourage you to join us in this prayer:

Dear Heavenly Father,
I praise You this day for Your goodness and mercy. At times I want to know why, but I recognize Your understanding is far beyond my own, and that Your Word is true. It is written that 'all things work together for good to those who are in You.' (Romans 8:28) It is hard to imagine at times what good could come from this death, but I choose to believe Your Word. Forgive me for my moments of anger and bitterness that may have been directed at You. I rededicate my life to You and want Your will to be done in my life and my family. I thank You for my salvation and the hope I have of spending an eternity with my child who is now in Your care. My offspring are a gift from You, and I place them in Your protection. Father, I know You understand my pain and loss. Heal my heart; replace my grief with joy. Holy Spirit, come and comfort me and fill this emptiness. Let me become a vessel that You can flow through. Strengthen me to share Your message of grace with others. Lord, let the testimony of my mouth be one of continuous praise to You, not only for

the good things you do for me, but simply because of Who You are! Lord, let the seed of this death produce life.

In Jesus' name I pray, Amen.

A current catalogue of books
written by Scott ♥ Cheri Scheer
is available online at

www.familyministries.net

Scott ♥ *Cheri Scheer*

Jarred & Rochelle Fenlason with their children
Jordan Scott and Carlye Dana